50 Easy Slow Cooker Dinners for Family Nights

By: Kelly Johnson

Table of Contents

- Beef Stroganoff
- Chicken Alfredo
- Pulled Pork Sandwiches
- Chili
- Chicken Tacos
- Beef and Vegetable Stew
- Chicken and Rice Casserole
- Pot Roast
- Sloppy Joes
- BBQ Ribs
- Chicken Parmesan
- Beef and Broccoli
- White Chicken Chili
- Meatball Subs
- Sweet and Sour Chicken
- Chicken and Dumplings
- Teriyaki Chicken
- Carnitas
- Beef Burritos
- Chicken Enchiladas
- Pulled Chicken Sandwiches
- Sausage and Peppers
- Chicken Pot Pie
- Shepherd's Pie
- Taco Soup
- Chicken Fajitas
- Beef Tacos
- Chicken Cacciatore
- Lasagna
- Beef Brisket
- Pork Carnitas Tacos
- Chicken and Sweet Potato Stew
- Vegetable Soup
- Chicken Tortilla Soup
- Beef Empanadas

- Chicken and Spinach Alfredo
- Meatball Stew
- BBQ Chicken
- Chicken Marsala
- Lemon Garlic Chicken
- Stuffed Bell Peppers
- Beef Chili Mac
- Sausage and Potato Bake
- Chicken and Black Bean Chili
- Pork Schnitzel
- Sweet and Spicy Chicken
- Baked Ziti
- Chicken Shawarma
- Pasta Primavera
- Pork and Sauerkraut

Beef Stroganoff

Ingredients:

- 500g beef tenderloin or sirloin, sliced into strips
- 1 onion, finely chopped
- 2 cloves garlic, minced
- 200g mushrooms, sliced
- 1 cup beef broth
- 1 tbsp Dijon mustard
- 1 tsp paprika
- 200ml sour cream
- 2 tbsp flour
- 2 tbsp butter
- Salt and pepper to taste

Instructions:

1. Heat butter in a skillet and sauté onions and garlic until soft.
2. Add beef strips and cook until browned.
3. Stir in mushrooms and cook until they release their moisture.
4. Sprinkle in flour and paprika, stir to combine.
5. Add beef broth and mustard, bring to a simmer.
6. Stir in sour cream, season with salt and pepper, and simmer for 5-10 minutes.
7. Serve over egg noodles or rice.

Chicken Alfredo

Ingredients:

- 500g chicken breasts, sliced
- 1 tbsp olive oil
- 4 cloves garlic, minced
- 200ml heavy cream
- 100g Parmesan cheese, grated
- 2 tbsp butter
- 350g fettuccine pasta
- Salt and pepper to taste

Instructions:

1. Cook the fettuccine pasta according to package instructions. Drain and set aside.
2. Heat olive oil in a pan, cook chicken until browned and cooked through. Remove from pan and set aside.
3. In the same pan, melt butter and sauté garlic until fragrant.
4. Pour in heavy cream and simmer for 5 minutes, then stir in Parmesan cheese.
5. Add chicken back to the pan, mix in the pasta, and season with salt and pepper.
6. Serve with extra Parmesan and parsley.

Pulled Pork Sandwiches

Ingredients:

- 1.5kg pork shoulder
- 1 onion, chopped
- 2 cloves garlic, minced
- 1 cup BBQ sauce
- 1 cup chicken broth
- 1 tbsp brown sugar
- 1 tsp paprika
- 1 tsp chili powder
- 1 tsp salt
- 1 tsp black pepper
- Buns for serving

Instructions:

1. Preheat the oven to 160°C (320°F). Rub the pork shoulder with paprika, chili powder, salt, and pepper.
2. In a roasting pan, place the pork, onion, garlic, and chicken broth. Cover tightly with foil and roast for 3-4 hours.
3. Shred the pork with two forks and mix with BBQ sauce and brown sugar.
4. Serve on buns with coleslaw, if desired.

Chili

Ingredients:

- 500g ground beef
- 1 onion, chopped
- 2 cloves garlic, minced
- 1 can (400g) diced tomatoes
- 1 can (400g) kidney beans, drained
- 1 can (400g) black beans, drained
- 1 can (150g) tomato paste
- 2 tbsp chili powder
- 1 tsp cumin
- 1 tsp paprika
- Salt and pepper to taste

Instructions:

1. Brown ground beef in a large pot, then remove excess fat.
2. Add onions and garlic, cook until softened.
3. Stir in diced tomatoes, beans, tomato paste, and spices.
4. Bring to a boil, reduce heat, and simmer for 30 minutes.
5. Serve with sour cream, cheese, or cornbread.

Chicken Tacos

Ingredients:

- 500g chicken breasts, cooked and shredded
- 1 packet taco seasoning
- ½ cup water
- 12 small taco shells
- 1 cup lettuce, shredded
- 1 cup cheese, grated
- 1 tomato, diced
- Salsa and sour cream for serving

Instructions:

1. Cook chicken breasts and shred them.
2. In a pan, combine chicken, taco seasoning, and water. Simmer until heated through.
3. Warm taco shells in the oven.
4. Fill taco shells with chicken and top with lettuce, cheese, tomato, salsa, and sour cream.

Beef and Vegetable Stew

Ingredients:

- 500g beef stew meat, cubed
- 3 carrots, peeled and sliced
- 3 potatoes, cubed
- 1 onion, chopped
- 2 cloves garlic, minced
- 4 cups beef broth
- 2 tbsp tomato paste
- 1 tsp thyme
- 1 tsp rosemary
- 2 tbsp olive oil
- Salt and pepper to taste

Instructions:

1. In a large pot, heat olive oil and brown beef in batches. Remove and set aside.
2. In the same pot, sauté onion and garlic until soft.
3. Stir in tomato paste, beef broth, thyme, rosemary, carrots, potatoes, and beef.
4. Bring to a boil, reduce heat, and simmer for 1-2 hours until tender.
5. Season with salt and pepper before serving.

Chicken and Rice Casserole

Ingredients:

- 500g chicken breasts, cooked and shredded
- 1 cup rice
- 1 can (400g) cream of chicken soup
- 1 cup chicken broth
- 1 onion, chopped
- 1 cup shredded cheese
- Salt and pepper to taste

Instructions:

1. Preheat the oven to 180°C (350°F).
2. In a large bowl, mix rice, soup, chicken broth, onions, and shredded chicken.
3. Transfer the mixture to a greased casserole dish and cover with foil.
4. Bake for 40 minutes, then uncover, sprinkle with cheese, and bake for an additional 10 minutes.

Pot Roast

Ingredients:

- 1.5kg beef roast (chuck roast or similar)
- 4 carrots, peeled and chopped
- 4 potatoes, chopped
- 1 onion, quartered
- 4 cloves garlic, smashed
- 2 cups beef broth
- 2 tbsp olive oil
- 1 tsp thyme
- Salt and pepper to taste

Instructions:

1. Preheat the oven to 160°C (320°F).
2. Heat olive oil in a Dutch oven and sear the beef on all sides.
3. Remove the beef and sauté onions and garlic until soft.
4. Return the beef to the pot, add broth, carrots, potatoes, thyme, salt, and pepper.
5. Cover and roast for 3-4 hours until the beef is tender.

Sloppy Joes

Ingredients:

- 500g ground beef
- 1 onion, chopped
- 1 bell pepper, chopped
- 1 can (400g) tomato sauce
- 2 tbsp Worcestershire sauce
- 2 tbsp brown sugar
- 1 tbsp mustard
- 4 hamburger buns
- Salt and pepper to taste

Instructions:

1. Brown ground beef in a skillet and drain excess fat.
2. Add onions and bell pepper, cook until softened.
3. Stir in tomato sauce, Worcestershire sauce, brown sugar, mustard, salt, and pepper.
4. Simmer for 10-15 minutes until thickened.
5. Serve on hamburger buns.

BBQ Ribs

Ingredients:

- 1 rack of baby back ribs
- 1 cup BBQ sauce
- 1 tbsp paprika
- 1 tsp garlic powder
- 1 tsp onion powder
- 1 tsp chili powder
- Salt and pepper to taste

Instructions:

1. Preheat the oven to 160°C (320°F).
2. Mix paprika, garlic powder, onion powder, chili powder, salt, and pepper. Rub this mixture onto the ribs.
3. Place the ribs on a baking sheet and cover with foil.
4. Roast for 2.5-3 hours until tender.
5. Brush with BBQ sauce and grill for 5-10 minutes until caramelized.

Chicken Parmesan

Ingredients:

- 4 chicken breasts, boneless and skinless
- 1 cup breadcrumbs
- 1 cup grated Parmesan cheese
- 2 eggs, beaten
- 1 cup marinara sauce
- 200g mozzarella cheese, shredded
- 2 tbsp olive oil
- Salt and pepper to taste
- Fresh basil for garnish

Instructions:

1. Preheat the oven to 180°C (350°F).
2. Mix breadcrumbs and Parmesan cheese. Season chicken with salt and pepper, then dip into the beaten eggs and coat with breadcrumb mixture.
3. Heat olive oil in a pan and brown the chicken on both sides.
4. Transfer chicken to a baking dish, top with marinara sauce and mozzarella.
5. Bake for 20 minutes, or until the cheese is melted and bubbly. Garnish with basil before serving.

Beef and Broccoli

Ingredients:

- 500g beef, sliced thinly (flank steak or sirloin)
- 2 cups broccoli florets
- 2 tbsp soy sauce
- 1 tbsp oyster sauce
- 2 tbsp brown sugar
- 1 tsp garlic, minced
- 1 tsp ginger, minced
- 1 tbsp cornstarch
- 1 tbsp vegetable oil
- Salt and pepper to taste

Instructions:

1. Heat oil in a pan, sauté garlic and ginger for 1 minute.
2. Add beef and cook until browned, then remove from the pan.
3. In the same pan, add soy sauce, oyster sauce, brown sugar, and cornstarch with a little water to create the sauce.
4. Add broccoli and cook until tender, then return the beef to the pan and stir to combine.
5. Season with salt and pepper, and serve over rice.

White Chicken Chili

Ingredients:

- 500g chicken breasts, cooked and shredded
- 1 onion, chopped
- 2 cloves garlic, minced
- 2 cans (400g) white beans, drained and rinsed
- 1 can (400g) green chilies
- 1 cup chicken broth
- 1 tsp cumin
- 1 tsp chili powder
- 1 tsp oregano
- ½ tsp salt
- 1 cup sour cream
- ½ cup shredded cheese

Instructions:

1. Sauté onions and garlic in a pot until soft.
2. Add chicken, beans, green chilies, chicken broth, cumin, chili powder, oregano, and salt. Bring to a boil, then simmer for 20 minutes.
3. Stir in sour cream and cheese, and cook for another 5 minutes.
4. Serve with extra cheese and tortilla chips.

Meatball Subs

Ingredients:

- 500g ground beef
- 1 egg
- 1/2 cup breadcrumbs
- 2 tbsp Parmesan cheese
- 1 tsp garlic powder
- 1 tsp dried oregano
- Salt and pepper to taste
- 1 jar marinara sauce
- 4 sub rolls
- 200g mozzarella cheese, shredded

Instructions:

1. Preheat the oven to 180°C (350°F).
2. Mix ground beef, egg, breadcrumbs, Parmesan, garlic powder, oregano, salt, and pepper. Form into meatballs.
3. Bake meatballs on a tray for 15 minutes.
4. Heat marinara sauce in a pan, add meatballs, and simmer for 10 minutes.
5. Toast sub rolls, then fill with meatballs, sauce, and mozzarella. Bake for 5-10 minutes until the cheese is melted.

Sweet and Sour Chicken

Ingredients:

- 500g chicken breast, cubed
- 1 onion, chopped
- 1 bell pepper, chopped
- 1 can (400g) pineapple chunks in juice
- 2 tbsp soy sauce
- 3 tbsp vinegar
- 3 tbsp ketchup
- 2 tbsp sugar
- 1 tbsp cornstarch mixed with 2 tbsp water

Instructions:

1. Heat oil in a pan, cook chicken until browned and set aside.
2. In the same pan, sauté onion and bell pepper.
3. Add pineapple, soy sauce, vinegar, ketchup, and sugar. Bring to a simmer.
4. Stir in the cornstarch mixture to thicken the sauce.
5. Return chicken to the pan, mix to coat, and serve with rice.

Chicken and Dumplings

Ingredients:

- 500g chicken breast, shredded
- 1 onion, chopped
- 2 carrots, chopped
- 2 celery stalks, chopped
- 4 cups chicken broth
- 2 cups milk
- 1 tsp thyme
- Salt and pepper to taste
- 1 cup all-purpose flour
- 1 tsp baking powder
- ½ tsp salt
- ½ cup milk (for dumplings)

Instructions:

1. In a pot, cook onion, carrots, and celery until soft.
2. Add chicken broth, milk, shredded chicken, thyme, salt, and pepper. Bring to a boil and simmer for 15 minutes.
3. In a bowl, mix flour, baking powder, salt, and milk to make the dumpling batter.
4. Drop spoonfuls of the batter into the soup. Cover and cook for 10 minutes until dumplings are cooked through.
5. Serve hot with a sprinkle of parsley.

Teriyaki Chicken

Ingredients:

- 500g chicken breast, sliced
- 2 tbsp soy sauce
- 2 tbsp honey
- 1 tbsp sesame oil
- 1 tbsp rice vinegar
- 2 cloves garlic, minced
- 1 tsp ginger, grated
- 1 tbsp sesame seeds (optional)
- Green onions for garnish

Instructions:

1. Mix soy sauce, honey, sesame oil, rice vinegar, garlic, and ginger in a bowl to make the marinade.
2. Marinate chicken for 30 minutes to 1 hour.
3. Cook chicken in a skillet until browned and cooked through.
4. Garnish with sesame seeds and green onions, and serve with rice or vegetables.

Carnitas

Ingredients:

- 1.5kg pork shoulder, cut into chunks
- 1 onion, chopped
- 4 cloves garlic, minced
- 1 tsp cumin
- 1 tsp chili powder
- 1 tsp oregano
- 2 bay leaves
- 2 cups orange juice
- Salt and pepper to taste

Instructions:

1. Season pork with cumin, chili powder, oregano, salt, and pepper.
2. Place pork, onion, garlic, bay leaves, and orange juice in a slow cooker.
3. Cook on low for 6-8 hours until the pork is tender and shreds easily.
4. Shred the pork with forks and serve on tortillas with your favorite toppings.

Beef Burritos

Ingredients:

- 500g ground beef
- 1 onion, chopped
- 1 packet taco seasoning
- 1 can (400g) refried beans
- 1 cup shredded cheese
- 8 flour tortillas
- Salsa and sour cream for serving

Instructions:

1. Cook ground beef and onions in a skillet until browned.
2. Add taco seasoning and follow package instructions.
3. Warm tortillas and spread a layer of refried beans on each.
4. Add beef mixture and top with cheese.
5. Roll up the tortillas and serve with salsa and sour cream.

Chicken Enchiladas

Ingredients:

- 500g chicken breasts, cooked and shredded
- 1 onion, chopped
- 1 can (400g) red enchilada sauce
- 8 corn tortillas
- 1 cup shredded cheese
- 1 tsp cumin
- 1 tsp chili powder
- 1 tbsp olive oil

Instructions:

1. Preheat the oven to 180°C (350°F).
2. Heat olive oil in a pan, sauté onions until soft, then stir in chicken, cumin, and chili powder.
3. Warm tortillas, then spoon chicken mixture into each and roll them up.
4. Place tortillas in a baking dish, cover with enchilada sauce and cheese.
5. Bake for 20-25 minutes until bubbly and golden.

Pulled Chicken Sandwiches

Ingredients:

- 500g chicken breasts
- 1 cup BBQ sauce
- 1 onion, chopped
- 2 cloves garlic, minced
- 1 tbsp olive oil
- 1 tsp paprika
- 1 tsp salt
- 1 tsp pepper
- 4 hamburger buns

Instructions:

1. Heat olive oil in a pan and sauté onion and garlic until softened.
2. Add chicken breasts, paprika, salt, pepper, and BBQ sauce. Simmer for 20-30 minutes until chicken is cooked through.
3. Shred the chicken with two forks and stir in more BBQ sauce if desired.
4. Serve on hamburger buns with coleslaw or pickles.

Sausage and Peppers

Ingredients:

- 4 sausages (Italian or your choice)
- 2 bell peppers, sliced
- 1 onion, sliced
- 2 cloves garlic, minced
- 1 tbsp olive oil
- 1 tsp dried oregano
- Salt and pepper to taste

Instructions:

1. Heat olive oil in a skillet and cook sausages until browned and cooked through. Remove and set aside.
2. In the same skillet, sauté garlic, onions, and bell peppers until softened.
3. Slice sausages and return them to the pan. Add oregano, salt, and pepper.
4. Cook for an additional 5-10 minutes, stirring occasionally. Serve on rolls or over rice.

Chicken Pot Pie

Ingredients:

For the filling:

- 500g cooked chicken, diced
- 1 cup frozen peas and carrots
- 1 onion, chopped
- 2 cloves garlic, minced
- 2 cups chicken broth
- 1 cup heavy cream
- 2 tbsp butter
- 2 tbsp flour
- Salt and pepper to taste

For the crust:

- 1 sheet puff pastry or pie dough
- 1 egg, beaten (for egg wash)

Instructions:

1. Preheat the oven to 200°C (400°F).
2. In a pan, melt butter and sauté onions and garlic until soft.
3. Stir in flour and cook for 1-2 minutes. Slowly add chicken broth and cream, stirring until thickened.
4. Add cooked chicken, peas, carrots, salt, and pepper.
5. Pour filling into a baking dish, top with pastry, and trim excess dough. Brush with egg wash.
6. Bake for 25-30 minutes until golden brown and bubbly.

Shepherd's Pie

Ingredients:

For the filling:

- 500g ground lamb (or beef for cottage pie)
- 1 onion, chopped
- 2 cloves garlic, minced
- 1 cup carrots, diced
- 1 cup peas
- 1 cup beef broth
- 1 tbsp Worcestershire sauce
- 1 tbsp tomato paste
- Salt and pepper to taste

For the mashed potatoes:

- 4 large potatoes, peeled and chopped
- 2 tbsp butter
- 1/2 cup milk
- Salt and pepper to taste

Instructions:

1. Preheat the oven to 180°C (350°F).
2. Boil potatoes until soft, then mash with butter, milk, salt, and pepper.
3. In a pan, cook ground lamb with onions and garlic until browned. Add carrots, peas, broth, Worcestershire sauce, tomato paste, salt, and pepper. Simmer for 10 minutes.
4. Transfer the filling to a baking dish, top with mashed potatoes, and bake for 20 minutes until the top is golden.

Taco Soup

Ingredients:

- 500g ground beef or turkey
- 1 onion, chopped
- 2 cloves garlic, minced
- 1 can (400g) black beans, drained
- 1 can (400g) corn kernels, drained
- 1 can (400g) diced tomatoes
- 1 packet taco seasoning
- 1 cup beef or chicken broth
- 1 tsp chili powder
- Salt and pepper to taste
- Sour cream, shredded cheese, and tortilla chips for garnish

Instructions:

1. In a large pot, cook ground meat, onions, and garlic until browned.
2. Add beans, corn, tomatoes, taco seasoning, chili powder, broth, salt, and pepper.
3. Bring to a boil, then simmer for 20 minutes.
4. Serve with sour cream, cheese, and tortilla chips.

Chicken Fajitas

Ingredients:

- 500g chicken breast, sliced
- 2 bell peppers, sliced
- 1 onion, sliced
- 2 cloves garlic, minced
- 2 tbsp olive oil
- 1 tbsp lime juice
- 1 tsp chili powder
- 1 tsp cumin
- 1 tsp paprika
- Salt and pepper to taste
- Flour tortillas for serving

Instructions:

1. Heat olive oil in a skillet and cook chicken until browned. Remove and set aside.
2. In the same skillet, sauté garlic, onions, and bell peppers until soft.
3. Add chicken back to the skillet with lime juice, chili powder, cumin, paprika, salt, and pepper.
4. Cook for another 5 minutes, stirring to combine.
5. Serve with warm tortillas and your favorite toppings.

Carnitas

Ingredients:

- 1.5kg pork shoulder, cut into chunks
- 1 onion, chopped
- 4 cloves garlic, minced
- 1 tsp cumin
- 1 tsp chili powder
- 1 tsp oregano
- 2 bay leaves
- 2 cups orange juice
- Salt and pepper to taste

Instructions:

1. Season pork with cumin, chili powder, oregano, salt, and pepper.
2. Place pork, onion, garlic, bay leaves, and orange juice in a slow cooker.
3. Cook on low for 6-8 hours until the pork is tender and shreds easily.
4. Shred the pork with two forks and serve on tortillas or in tacos.

Beef Burritos

Ingredients:

- 500g ground beef
- 1 packet taco seasoning
- 1 can (400g) refried beans
- 1 cup shredded cheese
- 8 flour tortillas
- Salsa and sour cream for serving

Instructions:

1. Cook ground beef in a skillet and add taco seasoning according to the packet instructions.
2. Warm tortillas and spread a layer of refried beans on each.
3. Add beef mixture and top with cheese.
4. Roll up the tortillas and serve with salsa and sour cream.

Chicken Enchiladas

Ingredients:

- 500g chicken breasts, cooked and shredded
- 1 onion, chopped
- 1 can (400g) red enchilada sauce
- 8 corn tortillas
- 1 cup shredded cheese
- 1 tsp cumin
- 1 tsp chili powder
- 1 tbsp olive oil

Instructions:

1. Preheat the oven to 180°C (350°F).
2. Heat olive oil in a pan, sauté onions until soft, then stir in chicken, cumin, and chili powder.
3. Warm tortillas, then spoon chicken mixture into each and roll them up.
4. Place tortillas in a baking dish, cover with enchilada sauce and cheese.
5. Bake for 20-25 minutes until bubbly and golden.

Beef Brisket

Ingredients:

- 1.5kg beef brisket
- 2 tbsp olive oil
- 1 onion, chopped
- 3 cloves garlic, minced
- 1 cup beef broth
- 1 cup red wine
- 2 tbsp tomato paste
- 1 tbsp Worcestershire sauce
- 1 tsp thyme
- 1 tsp rosemary
- Salt and pepper to taste

Instructions:

1. Preheat the oven to 160°C (320°F).
2. Heat olive oil in a large pot and sear brisket on all sides until browned. Remove and set aside.
3. Sauté onions and garlic in the same pot until softened.
4. Stir in tomato paste, Worcestershire sauce, thyme, rosemary, beef broth, and wine.
5. Return the brisket to the pot, cover with foil, and cook for 3-4 hours until tender.
6. Let the brisket rest before slicing and serving with the sauce.

Pork Carnitas Tacos

Ingredients:

- 1.5kg pork shoulder, cut into chunks
- 1 onion, chopped
- 4 cloves garlic, minced
- 1 tbsp cumin
- 1 tbsp chili powder
- 2 bay leaves
- 2 cups orange juice
- 1 lime, juiced
- 8 small tortillas
- Salsa and cilantro for serving

Instructions:

1. Season the pork with cumin, chili powder, salt, and pepper.
2. Place the pork, onion, garlic, bay leaves, orange juice, and lime juice in a slow cooker.
3. Cook on low for 6-8 hours until the pork is tender and easily shreds.
4. Shred the pork with two forks and serve in tortillas with salsa and cilantro.

Chicken and Sweet Potato Stew

Ingredients:

- 500g chicken thighs, boneless and skinless, cubed
- 2 medium sweet potatoes, peeled and cubed
- 1 onion, chopped
- 2 cloves garlic, minced
- 1 can (400g) diced tomatoes
- 4 cups chicken broth
- 1 tsp paprika
- 1 tsp cumin
- 1 tsp thyme
- Salt and pepper to taste

Instructions:

1. Heat olive oil in a large pot, brown the chicken cubes, and set aside.
2. In the same pot, sauté onions and garlic until softened.
3. Add sweet potatoes, diced tomatoes, chicken broth, and spices.
4. Bring to a simmer, then cook for 30 minutes until the sweet potatoes are tender and the chicken is fully cooked.
5. Serve hot with a garnish of fresh parsley.

Vegetable Soup

Ingredients:

- 2 tbsp olive oil
- 1 onion, chopped
- 2 carrots, chopped
- 2 celery stalks, chopped
- 2 potatoes, cubed
- 1 zucchini, chopped
- 1 can (400g) diced tomatoes
- 4 cups vegetable broth
- 1 tsp thyme
- 1 tsp basil
- Salt and pepper to taste

Instructions:

1. Heat olive oil in a large pot and sauté onions, carrots, and celery until softened.
2. Add potatoes, zucchini, diced tomatoes, vegetable broth, thyme, and basil.
3. Bring to a boil, then simmer for 30 minutes, or until the vegetables are tender.
4. Season with salt and pepper and serve with crusty bread.

Chicken Tortilla Soup

Ingredients:

- 500g chicken breast, cooked and shredded
- 1 onion, chopped
- 2 cloves garlic, minced
- 1 can (400g) diced tomatoes
- 1 can (400g) black beans, drained
- 1 can (300g) corn kernels, drained
- 4 cups chicken broth
- 1 tsp cumin
- 1 tsp chili powder
- 1 tsp paprika
- 1 lime, juiced
- Tortilla chips, shredded cheese, and cilantro for garnish

Instructions:

1. Heat olive oil in a large pot and sauté onions and garlic until softened.
2. Stir in cumin, chili powder, paprika, and cook for 1 minute.
3. Add chicken, diced tomatoes, black beans, corn, and chicken broth. Bring to a simmer.
4. Simmer for 20-25 minutes, then stir in lime juice.
5. Serve with tortilla chips, cheese, and cilantro.

Beef Empanadas

Ingredients:

- 500g ground beef
- 1 onion, chopped
- 1 clove garlic, minced
- 1 tsp cumin
- 1 tsp paprika
- 1 tsp chili powder
- 1 egg (for egg wash)
- 12 empanada dough discs (store-bought or homemade)
- Salt and pepper to taste

Instructions:

1. Preheat the oven to 200°C (400°F).
2. Cook ground beef, onions, and garlic in a skillet until browned. Stir in cumin, paprika, chili powder, salt, and pepper.
3. Let the beef mixture cool, then spoon a small amount onto each dough disc.
4. Fold the discs over the filling, sealing the edges with a fork. Brush with egg wash.
5. Bake for 20-25 minutes until golden brown and crispy.

Chicken and Spinach Alfredo

Ingredients:

- 500g chicken breasts, sliced
- 1 onion, chopped
- 2 cloves garlic, minced
- 200g fresh spinach
- 200g fettuccine pasta
- 200ml heavy cream
- 100g Parmesan cheese, grated
- 1 tbsp olive oil
- Salt and pepper to taste

Instructions:

1. Cook fettuccine pasta according to package instructions.
2. Heat olive oil in a pan, cook chicken until browned, and set aside.
3. In the same pan, sauté onion and garlic until soft, then stir in spinach until wilted.
4. Add heavy cream, bring to a simmer, then stir in Parmesan cheese.
5. Add cooked chicken and pasta to the pan, toss to combine. Serve with extra cheese.

Meatball Stew

Ingredients:

For the meatballs:

- 500g ground beef
- 1 egg
- ½ cup breadcrumbs
- 1 tsp garlic powder
- 1 tsp onion powder
- Salt and pepper to taste

For the stew:

- 1 onion, chopped
- 2 carrots, sliced
- 3 potatoes, cubed
- 1 can (400g) diced tomatoes
- 4 cups beef broth
- 1 tsp thyme
- Salt and pepper to taste

Instructions:

1. Preheat the oven to 180°C (350°F). Mix all meatball ingredients and form into small balls.
2. Bake meatballs for 20-25 minutes until cooked through.
3. In a large pot, sauté onions and carrots until softened.
4. Add potatoes, tomatoes, beef broth, thyme, salt, and pepper, and bring to a simmer.
5. Add the baked meatballs to the stew and simmer for an additional 20 minutes. Serve hot.

BBQ Chicken

Ingredients:

- 4 chicken breasts or thighs
- 1 cup BBQ sauce
- 1 tbsp olive oil
- Salt and pepper to taste

Instructions:

1. Preheat the grill or oven to medium heat.
2. Brush chicken with olive oil and season with salt and pepper.
3. Grill chicken for 6-8 minutes on each side, until cooked through.
4. During the last few minutes, brush with BBQ sauce and cook for another 2 minutes.
5. Serve hot with extra BBQ sauce on the side.

Chicken Marsala

Ingredients:

- 4 chicken breasts, boneless and skinless
- 1 cup all-purpose flour
- 2 tbsp olive oil
- 1 cup Marsala wine
- 1 cup chicken broth
- 1 cup mushrooms, sliced
- 2 cloves garlic, minced
- 1 tbsp butter
- Salt and pepper to taste
- Fresh parsley for garnish

Instructions:

1. Season chicken breasts with salt and pepper, then dredge in flour.
2. Heat olive oil in a pan and brown the chicken on both sides. Remove and set aside.
3. In the same pan, sauté garlic and mushrooms until tender.
4. Add Marsala wine and chicken broth, simmer for 10 minutes.
5. Stir in butter and return the chicken to the pan. Cook for another 10 minutes until the chicken is cooked through.
6. Garnish with parsley and serve with mashed potatoes or pasta.

Lemon Garlic Chicken

Ingredients:

- 4 chicken breasts
- 2 tbsp olive oil
- 3 cloves garlic, minced
- 1 lemon, zest and juice
- 1 tsp dried thyme
- Salt and pepper to taste
- Fresh parsley for garnish

Instructions:

1. In a bowl, mix olive oil, garlic, lemon juice, zest, thyme, salt, and pepper.
2. Marinate chicken in the mixture for at least 30 minutes.
3. Heat olive oil in a pan and cook the chicken for 6-8 minutes on each side until cooked through.
4. Garnish with fresh parsley and serve with rice or vegetables.

Stuffed Bell Peppers

Ingredients:

- 4 large bell peppers, tops cut off and seeds removed
- 500g ground beef or turkey
- 1 cup cooked rice
- 1 can (400g) diced tomatoes
- 1 small onion, chopped
- 2 cloves garlic, minced
- 1 tsp cumin
- 1 tsp paprika
- 1 tsp dried oregano
- 1 cup shredded cheese (cheddar or mozzarella)
- Salt and pepper to taste

Instructions:

1. Preheat the oven to 180°C (350°F).
2. In a pan, cook ground meat with onions and garlic until browned.
3. Stir in diced tomatoes, rice, cumin, paprika, oregano, salt, and pepper.
4. Stuff the bell peppers with the meat mixture and place them in a baking dish.
5. Top with cheese and bake for 25-30 minutes until the peppers are tender.

Beef Chili Mac

Ingredients:

- 500g ground beef
- 1 onion, chopped
- 2 cloves garlic, minced
- 1 can (400g) diced tomatoes
- 1 can (400g) kidney beans, drained
- 1 cup beef broth
- 2 tsp chili powder
- 1 tsp cumin
- 200g elbow macaroni
- 1 cup shredded cheese (cheddar or Mexican blend)
- Salt and pepper to taste

Instructions:

1. Cook elbow macaroni according to package instructions, then set aside.
2. In a large pan, brown ground beef with onions and garlic.
3. Add diced tomatoes, kidney beans, beef broth, chili powder, cumin, salt, and pepper.
4. Simmer for 20 minutes.
5. Stir in cooked macaroni and top with cheese. Cook for another 5 minutes until the cheese melts.
6. Serve hot with sour cream or extra cheese.

Sausage and Potato Bake

Ingredients:

- 500g sausage links (Italian or breakfast sausage)
- 4 medium potatoes, peeled and chopped
- 1 onion, chopped
- 2 cloves garlic, minced
- 2 tbsp olive oil
- 1 tsp rosemary
- 1 tsp thyme
- Salt and pepper to taste

Instructions:

1. Preheat the oven to 180°C (350°F).
2. In a large baking dish, toss potatoes, onions, garlic, rosemary, thyme, salt, and pepper with olive oil.
3. Arrange sausage links on top of the vegetables.
4. Bake for 40-45 minutes, turning sausages halfway through, until the sausages are cooked through and potatoes are tender.
5. Slice sausages before serving with the roasted vegetables.

Chicken and Black Bean Chili

Ingredients:

- 500g chicken breast, cooked and shredded
- 1 can (400g) black beans, drained and rinsed
- 1 can (400g) diced tomatoes
- 1 onion, chopped
- 2 cloves garlic, minced
- 1 tsp chili powder
- 1 tsp cumin
- 1 tsp paprika
- 1 cup chicken broth
- Salt and pepper to taste
- Sour cream, cilantro, and shredded cheese for garnish

Instructions:

1. In a large pot, sauté onions and garlic until soft.
2. Add shredded chicken, black beans, diced tomatoes, chili powder, cumin, paprika, salt, and pepper.
3. Pour in chicken broth and bring to a simmer.
4. Cook for 30 minutes, stirring occasionally.
5. Serve with sour cream, cilantro, and cheese on top.

Pork Schnitzel

Ingredients:

- 4 pork chops, boneless
- 1 cup all-purpose flour
- 2 eggs, beaten
- 1 cup breadcrumbs
- 1 tsp paprika
- 1 tsp garlic powder
- 1 tsp salt
- ½ tsp pepper
- 2 tbsp olive oil
- Lemon wedges for serving

Instructions:

1. Preheat the oven to 180°C (350°F).
2. Season pork chops with salt, pepper, garlic powder, and paprika.
3. Dredge the pork chops in flour, then dip in beaten eggs, and coat with breadcrumbs.
4. Heat olive oil in a pan over medium heat and fry the pork schnitzels for 4-5 minutes on each side until golden brown.
5. Transfer to a baking sheet and bake for 5-7 minutes to ensure they're cooked through.
6. Serve with lemon wedges and a side of potatoes or salad.

Sweet and Spicy Chicken

Ingredients:

- 500g chicken thighs, boneless and skinless
- 2 tbsp olive oil
- 2 tbsp honey
- 2 tbsp soy sauce
- 1 tbsp sriracha sauce
- 2 cloves garlic, minced
- 1 tbsp rice vinegar
- 1 tsp sesame oil
- Salt and pepper to taste
- Sesame seeds for garnish

Instructions:

1. Heat olive oil in a skillet over medium-high heat. Season chicken with salt and pepper.
2. Cook the chicken for 5-6 minutes on each side until golden and cooked through.
3. In a small bowl, mix honey, soy sauce, sriracha, garlic, rice vinegar, and sesame oil.
4. Pour the sauce over the chicken, stirring to coat evenly. Simmer for 3-5 minutes until the sauce thickens.
5. Garnish with sesame seeds and serve with rice or vegetables.

Baked Ziti

Ingredients:

- 500g ziti pasta
- 500g ground beef or Italian sausage
- 1 onion, chopped
- 2 cloves garlic, minced
- 1 jar (700g) marinara sauce
- 1 tsp Italian seasoning
- 1 tsp basil
- 1 cup ricotta cheese
- 2 cups shredded mozzarella cheese
- ½ cup grated Parmesan cheese

Instructions:

1. Preheat the oven to 180°C (350°F).
2. Cook ziti pasta according to package instructions, then drain.
3. In a skillet, cook ground beef or sausage with onions and garlic until browned.
4. Stir in marinara sauce, Italian seasoning, and basil. Simmer for 10 minutes.
5. Mix ricotta cheese with the cooked pasta, then layer with sauce in a baking dish.
6. Top with mozzarella and Parmesan cheese, then bake for 20 minutes until bubbly and golden.

Chicken Shawarma

Ingredients:

- 500g chicken breast or thighs, cut into strips
- 1 tbsp olive oil
- 1 tsp cumin
- 1 tsp paprika
- 1 tsp turmeric
- 1 tsp cinnamon
- 1 tsp garlic powder
- 1 tbsp lemon juice
- 1 tsp salt
- 1 tsp black pepper
- Pita bread for serving
- Tahini sauce for drizzling (optional)

Instructions:

1. In a bowl, mix olive oil, cumin, paprika, turmeric, cinnamon, garlic powder, lemon juice, salt, and pepper.
2. Toss chicken in the marinade and let sit for at least 30 minutes.
3. Heat a skillet over medium heat and cook the chicken for 5-7 minutes until browned and cooked through.
4. Serve the chicken in pita bread with vegetables and drizzle with tahini sauce if desired.

Pasta Primavera

Ingredients:

- 350g pasta (penne, fusilli, or spaghetti)
- 1 zucchini, sliced
- 1 bell pepper, chopped
- 1 cup cherry tomatoes, halved
- 1 cup broccoli florets
- 2 cloves garlic, minced
- 2 tbsp olive oil
- 1 tsp Italian seasoning
- ½ cup Parmesan cheese, grated
- Salt and pepper to taste

Instructions:

1. Cook pasta according to package instructions, then drain.
2. In a large pan, heat olive oil and sauté garlic, zucchini, bell pepper, cherry tomatoes, and broccoli for 5-7 minutes until tender.
3. Add Italian seasoning, salt, and pepper.
4. Toss the cooked pasta with the vegetables and sprinkle with Parmesan cheese. Serve with extra cheese if desired.

Pork and Sauerkraut

Ingredients:

- 1.5kg pork shoulder, boneless
- 2 cups sauerkraut, drained
- 1 onion, sliced
- 2 cloves garlic, minced
- 1 cup chicken broth
- 1 tbsp caraway seeds (optional)
- 2 tbsp olive oil
- Salt and pepper to taste

Instructions:

1. Preheat the oven to 160°C (320°F).
2. Season pork shoulder with salt and pepper.
3. In a Dutch oven, heat olive oil and brown the pork on all sides.
4. Remove the pork and sauté onions and garlic until soft.
5. Add sauerkraut, chicken broth, and caraway seeds, then return the pork to the pot.
6. Cover and roast for 3-4 hours until the pork is tender. Serve with mashed potatoes or bread.